NFL TODAY $16.95   31 Titles

Arizona Cardinals	Minnesota Vikings
Atlanta Falcons	New England Patriots
Baltimore Ravens	New Orleans Saints
Buffalo Bills	New York Giants
Carolina Panthers	New York Jets
Chicago Bears	Oakland Raiders
Cincinnati Bengals	Philadelphia Eagles
Cleveland Browns	Pittsburgh Steelers
Dallas Cowboys	St. Louis Rams
Denver Broncos	San Diego Chargers
Detroit Lions	San Francisco 49ers
Green Bay Packers	Seattle Seahawks
Indianapolis Colts	Tampa Bay Buccaneers
Jacksonville Jaguars	Tennessee Titans
Kansas City Chiefs	Washington Redskins
Miami Dolphins	

CREATIVE EDUCATION

SEATTLE SEAHAWKS

SEATTLE TODAY

JULIE NELSON

Published by Creative Education
123 South Broad Street, Mankato, Minnesota 56001
Creative Education is an imprint of The Creative Company

Designed by Rita Marshall

Photos by: Allsport USA, SportsChrome

Library of Congress Cataloging-in-Publication Data

Nelson, Julie.
Seattle Seahawks / by Julie Nelson.
p. cm. — (NFL today)
Summary: Traces the history of the team from its beginnings through 1999.
ISBN 1-58341-060-0

1. Seattle Seahawks (Football team)—History—Juvenile literature. [1. Seattle
Seahawks (Football team)—History. 2. Football—History.] I. Title.
II. Series: NFL today (Mankato, Minn.)

GV956.S4N45   2000
796.332'64'09797772—dc21   99-015759

First edition

9 8 7 6 5 4 3 2 1

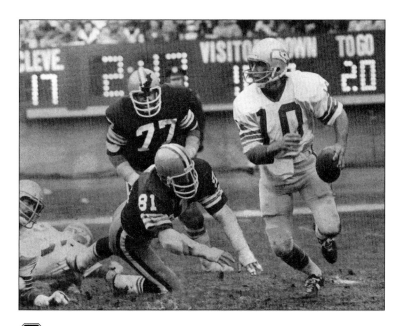

Seattle, Washington, has been called the most livable city in the United States. The "Emerald City," as it is known, offers its residents a unique combination of business, culture, and a spectacular natural environment. Aerospace and computer companies have set up their headquarters in Seattle; goods to and from the Far East often pass through the city's port; local opera and theater companies are among the country's finest; and numerous Seattle-based rock musicians have burst upon the national scene in the last decade.

Then there are the natural wonders, such as Puget Sound to the west, Lake Washington to the east, and the lofty

Mount Rainier, which dominates the southeastern skies. Within this beautiful environment, Seattle has emerged as the population and trade center of the Pacific Northwest.

Seattle has also become a mecca for sports fans living in the region. By the 1970s, professional franchises in baseball, basketball, and football were established there, and all three sports have built a strong following of loyal fans over the past few decades.

No franchise, however, has taken Seattle fans on the kind of roller-coaster ride that the Seahawks of the National Football League have. From the team's beginning to today, the Seahawks have always been exciting and unpredictable. Maybe that's why the team has developed such a strong bond with its fans, a bond that makes the Seahawks one of the best-supported franchises in the NFL.

THE EXPANSION YEARS: ZORN TO BE WILD

In 1974, when the NFL granted Seattle an expansion franchise to begin play during the 1976 season, the team's owners decided to hold a public contest to choose a name that fit the city and the sport. After more than 20,000 suggestions were submitted, a winner was decided: the "Seahawks," in honor of a large, swift, and powerful bird native to the coastal area.

The Seahawks would play their home games in the Kingdome, the city's new 65,000-seat indoor stadium designed to house both football and baseball. Long before the Seahawks' first game, tickets were a hot item, and fans quickly snapped up all of the season tickets available.

Devastating tackler Chad Brown.

1 9 7 8

Jim Zorn, the AFC's leading passer, also ran for 290 yards and six touchdowns.

All 65,000 Kingdome seats were filled when the Seahawks played their first preseason game against the San Francisco 49ers on August 1, 1976. Although the Seahawks fell 27–20, none of the fans left the Kingdome depressed. In fact, they didn't leave at all for a few minutes. Instead, they rose and gave the team a long standing ovation that was both a cheer and a welcome to the Pacific Northwest.

Many of the cheers were for Jim Zorn, a quarterback who had been rejected by other NFL teams but found a home in Seattle. Zorn wasn't drafted by the Seahawks or any other team when he graduated from a little-known college named Cal Poly–Pomona in 1975. He hooked on with the Dallas Cowboys as a free agent but spent most of the 1975 season on the sidelines recovering from injuries. After the Cowboys released him, Zorn convinced Seahawks coach Jack Patera to give him a tryout.

Zorn faced long odds against making the Seahawks' roster when he arrived at the club's first training camp. There were eight other quarterbacks in camp—several with NFL experience. Zorn's only experience had come from watching the Cowboys practice.

Zorn handled the job of quarterback differently than most players. He didn't just drop back and throw the ball. He'd drop back, and when plays broke down, he'd take off running. During summer vacations in high school, Zorn once explained, he would run on a local baseball field and throw the football at the metal backstop. Through that drill, he worked on both his throwing accuracy and his moves as a runner.

Some pro scouts thought Zorn was too wild and unpredictable. But that was the secret to his success. During that first preseason with the Seahawks, the other quarterbacks tried using the usual methods. Zorn did the unusual—and succeeded. Coach Patera had his quarterback, and Seattle fans had a unique football star.

Seattle opened its first regular season against the St. Louis Cardinals, and Zorn almost pulled off the upset. The expansion Seahawks, a collection of rookies and castoffs from other teams, battled the Cardinals (who had made the playoffs two years in a row) down to the wire before losing 30–24. The Seahawks came close to beating Green Bay a few weeks later, and then faced off against the other expansion club, the Tampa Bay Buccaneers, in week six. In that game, Seattle claimed its first NFL victory 13–10 in another close contest.

Efren Herrera set a team record for kicking accuracy, making 19 of 23 field goals.

The Seahawks' opening season ended with a 2–12 record. Zorn threw for more than 2,500 yards, Sherman Smith led the team in rushing with 537 yards, and a young receiver named Steve Largent began his Hall of Fame career with 54 receptions for 705 yards and four touchdowns.

The following year, the Seahawks set an NFL second-year record with five victories and finished ahead of the veteran Kansas City Chiefs in the AFC Western Division. The club was on its way up.

STEVE LARGENT: A GENUINE HERO

By 1978, the passing combination of Jim Zorn to Steve Largent had become one of the most successful in the league. The two players seemed to be communicating on their own special wave length, and they drove opposing defenses crazy. Zorn topped the AFC with 248 completions for

Hall of Fame receiver Steve Largent.

Fearless running back Curt Warner.

3,283 yards, and Largent grabbed a league-leading 71 passes for 1,168 yards—the first of a record eight 1,000-yard seasons for Largent.

The dynamic duo also helped the Seahawks establish the club's first winning record in only its third year in the league. Seattle ended the 1978 campaign at 9–7, finishing second in the AFC West.

The highlight of the year was Seattle's first appearance before a national television audience on Monday Night Football. After the nervous Seahawks fell behind the host Atlanta Falcons 14–0, Seattle turned on the afterburners. Zorn threw passes to everyone, including one to kicker Efren Herrera on a fake field goal. The Seahawks even successfully captured an onside kick that turned into a quick score. When the dust settled, the Seahawks had won not only the game, 31–28, but also the respect of football fans across the country.

On a team of unusual players with unusual backgrounds, Largent fit right in. Unlike Zorn, Largent actually had been drafted, but not by the Seahawks. In the fourth round of the 1976 NFL draft, the Houston Oilers took Largent. Then, during the preseason, the Oilers traded him to Seattle for a future draft pick.

Thirteen years after that trade, Largent retired owning every important NFL pass-receiving record and having earned a place in the Pro Football Hall of Fame. Though he wasn't fast, and he didn't look particularly graceful on the field, Largent did have great quickness. He could change directions instantly and knew how to adjust pass routes to get to the ball.

Lester Hayes, a former All-Pro cornerback with the Oakland Raiders, said, "Largent didn't look like a receiver. He

1 9 8 0

Middle linebacker Terry Beeson was a terror, making 101 total tackles.

looked like an insurance salesman. I thought I should be able to dominate this guy. But I never covered anybody who gave me as many problems as Steve Largent did."

Fred Biletnikoff, another Hall of Fame receiver, had an explanation for Largent's success. "I've never seen anyone spend more time at preparation," he said. "Steve Largent is a role model not just for kids, but for NFL players everywhere. Few if any had his dedication."

Largent helped make Jim Zorn and other Seattle quarterbacks look good from 1976 until 1989. When he retired, he was the NFL's career leader in receptions (819), receiving yards (13,089), touchdowns (100), consecutive games with a reception (177), 50-catch seasons (10), and 1,000-yard seasons (8). Although many of Largent's records have since been broken, his place in NFL history is secure.

Halfback Curt Warner set a new Seahawks record with 1,449 total rushing yards.

Largent was a role model off the field as well. The NFL named him "Man of the Year" in 1988 for his many activities in the Seattle community, particularly his efforts to raise funds to combat spina bifida, a crippling birth defect that affected one of his children. Recognizing Largent's special qualities, the Seahawks also created an award in his honor after his retirement. Since 1989, the Steve Largent Award is given each year to the Seattle player who "best exemplifies the spirit, dedication, and integrity of the Seattle Seahawks."

Largent continued to play a major role in his community even after his playing days. In 1994, he was elected to the U.S. House of Representatives from his home district in Tulsa, Oklahoma. "I am going to try to do something and make a difference," he said after his election. "This is the same way I got involved with the NFL. I took advantage of an opportunity."

1 9 8 5

Defensive end Jacob Green continued to dominate as a pass rusher, making 13.5 sacks.

Two winning campaigns in 1978 and 1979, spearheaded by Largent and Zorn, marked the high point of the Seahawks' first lap on the NFL rollercoaster. But in 1980, the club lost all eight of its home games and tumbled back to the bottom of the AFC West. The year's main highlight was the arrival of rookie defensive end Jacob Green from Texas A&M. Over the next 12 seasons, Green would anchor the Seahawks' defense, finishing his career among the all-time league leaders with 116 sacks.

In 1981, Seattle bounced back somewhat with a 6–10 record but still wound up last in its five-team division. Second-year man Dave Krieg replaced an injured Zorn at quarterback. The next year, Zorn was back, but the season was halted when players went on strike for seven weeks. During the strike, Jack Patera, the only head coach in Seahawks history, was fired. Team president Mike McCormack took over until the end of the year while he searched for the right man to put Seattle back on track.

McCormack soon selected Chuck Knox for the job. In Buffalo, Knox had turned a declining Bills franchise into a winner once again. He believed that a victorious team was one that combined a strong running game, a mistake-free offense, and a punishing defense that could cause turnovers.

Knox immediately established three priorities for the Seahawks: first, to pick up an outstanding running back; second, to find a quarterback who didn't gamble as much or throw as many interceptions as Jim Zorn; and third, to add some aggressive defensive players.

Pro-Bowl running back Chris Warren.

Outstanding defensive end Jacob Green.

The first need was met during the 1983 NFL draft. Seattle made a daring trade with the Houston Oilers, exchanging three high draft choices for Houston's first-round pick in the draft, the third choice overall. Knox used the pick to select running back Curt Warner, who had led his Penn State team to the college national championship in 1982. The Seahawks had their star running back.

By the middle of the 1983 season, Knox was ready to solve his quarterback problem, too. Zorn began the year as Seattle's starter, but the club got off to a sluggish start. In the eighth game of the season, the Seahawks were getting manhandled 24–0 by the Pittsburgh Steelers. At the start of the second half, Knox sent in Dave Krieg, his backup quarterback, and suddenly the team's whole attitude seemed to change. Krieg tossed two touchdown passes, played error-free, and nearly pulled out a victory.

Despite the 27–21 loss, the Seahawks were a changed club. They went 5–3 during the second half of the season, winning three of their last four games. The team's 9–7 record was good enough to earn Seattle its first trip to the playoffs.

Dave Krieg saw the playoffs as a chance to prove that he was the right man to lead the Seahawks. Krieg had been backing up Zorn for four seasons, getting a chance to play only when Zorn was injured. Few football experts—and even fewer fans—had heard of Krieg before Seattle's near comeback in 1983. He didn't have the quickest feet or the strongest arm, and he hailed from a tiny school—Milton College in Wisconsin—that actually closed down a few years after he left. Yet somehow, Krieg became one of the highest-rated passers in NFL history.

1 9 8 7

Quarterback Dave Krieg completed more than 60 percent of his passes.

The Seahawks prepare for battle along the line (pages 18-19).

1 9 8 8

Star safety Eugene Robinson led Seattle in tackles (114) for the first of two straight seasons.

Dave Krieg had some special qualities that helped him to overcome his lack of sheer physical talent. Guard Reggie McKenzie, who blocked for Krieg in Seattle for several years, explained, "Dave Krieg is one of those natural-born leader types. He comes into a game all jacked-up. His enthusiasm spills over and splashes on everyone else."

Krieg and his teammates were really pumped up on Christmas Eve, 1983, when they faced off against the Denver Broncos in the first round of the playoffs. Curt Warner gained 99 yards, Krieg was nearly perfect—completing 12 of 13 passes for 200 yards—and the Seahawks romped, 31–7. It was a great Christmas present for their fans.

The club had an even better New Year's gift in mind the following week, when Seattle traveled to Miami to take on the heavily favored Dolphins. No one thought the Seahawks had much of a chance; one Miami writer even insultingly referred to them as the "Sea-Whos."

Miami led the "Sea-Whos" 20–17 in the fourth quarter. But Krieg then engineered an impressive drive, hitting Largent with two key passes and then handing off to Warner for a touchdown that put Seattle on top for good. The Seahawks added a field goal to win 27–20. Unbelievably, the Seahawks would be facing the Los Angeles Raiders one week later for the AFC championship.

Chuck Knox was one of the few Seahawks who had any experience in conference title games. The coach had led the Rams to four NFC championship games and one Super Bowl appearance. Unfortunately, the Seahawks would end up one step short. Neither Krieg nor Zorn could get Seattle going, and the final score was a disappointing 30–7.

Zorn's departure a year later meant that Krieg was totally in charge of the Seahawks' offense, and he made the most of his opportunity, leading the club to a 12–4 record in 1984 and another playoff berth.

Coach Knox was most proud, however, of his team's improved defense. Led by ends Jacob Green and Jeff Bryant, safety Kenny Easley, and linebacker Keith Butler, the Seahawks' defensive unit made life miserable for opponents. Seattle posted a league-leading three shutouts in 1984.

In the playoffs, the Seahawks avenged the loss they'd suffered the year before to the Raiders with a 13–7 first-round win. Soon after, though, they fell victim to revenge themselves, as Miami crushed Seattle 31–10, ending its Super Bowl hopes once again.

Bryan Millard anchored the Seahawks' offensive line for the seventh straight season.

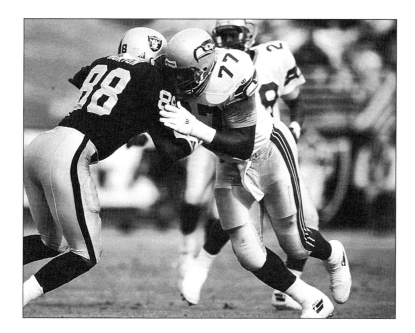

Relentless defensive lineman Jeff Bryant.

Few defenders could match receiver Joey Galloway's speed.

The Seahawks continued to play winning football over the next few seasons, though they never came close to a Super Bowl appearance. The team just missed the playoffs in 1986 and lost in the first round as a Wild Card in 1987. Throughout those years, Seattle fans could always count on Curt Warner gaining 1,000 or more yards a season, Steve Largent catching a pass in every game in which he played, and Jacob Green terrifying quarterbacks with his relentless pass rush.

1 9 9 1

Chuck Knox spent his final season in Seattle, leaving with a coaching record of 80–63.

Several other key players also arrived in the next few years. These included halfbacks John L. Williams and Chris Warren, defensive back Eugene Robinson, and wide receiver Brian Blades, who became the only Seahawks player other than Largent to gain 1,000 receiving yards in a season.

Of all these new players, Williams made the most sudden impact, earning a special place in Seattle history during the final game of the 1988 season. The Seahawks needed to beat their archrivals, the Los Angeles Raiders, to win a playoff spot and their first AFC West title. Williams made sure they didn't lose. He rushed for 59 yards and amassed 180 more yards on pass receptions, including a 75-yard touchdown scamper on a screen pass, to key a 43–37 Seattle victory.

The Seahawks had their first division championship, but their joy was short-lived. They fell once again in the first round of the playoffs, this time to the Super Bowl-bound Cincinnati Bengals.

In 1989 and 1991, Seattle failed to reach even a .500 record. Following a 7–9 campaign in 1991, Chuck Knox was fired. His replacement was former team president Tom Flores, who had previously led the Raiders to a Super Bowl victory in 1980. But even Flores's experience and talent could not halt the club's downward slide. The Seahawks fell to 2–14 in 1992, their worst record since their first year in the league. The one bright spot was the running of third-year halfback Chris Warren, who recorded the first of four straight seasons with at least 1,000 rushing yards.

Tackle Cortez Kennedy made 14 sacks—the third-highest total in team history.

FROM MIRER TO MOON

There was one other good thing about the Seahawks' otherwise terrible 1992 season. Seattle earned the right to pick second in the NFL draft and selected outstanding quar-

One of the NFL's best pass rushers, Michael Sinclair.

terback Rick Mirer from Notre Dame. Flores liked what he saw in the young man and made him the team's starting quarterback immediately.

Mirer responded with a terrific rookie year, completing 274 passes for 2,833 yards, breaking an NFL rookie record set by Jim Zorn in 1976. Mirer showed courage behind the Seahawks' porous offensive line, and although he was sacked 47 times, he never stayed down for long. "He is as tough a quarterback as I ever coached," Flores said.

1 9 9 5

Receiver Brian Blades caught passes for more than 1,000 yards.

Despite Mirer's solid performance, the Seahawks suffered back-to-back 6–10 seasons, and Flores was dismissed at the end of 1994. Team owner Tom Behring hired successful longtime college coach Dennis Erickson to replace Flores. Upon arriving in Seattle, Erickson designed a new passing attack around Rick Mirer and speedy wide receivers Brian Blades, Ricky Proehl, and Joey Galloway. The Seahawks' wide-open passing game, combined with Warren's rushing, put them back on the winning track. Only a season finale loss to the powerful Kansas City Chiefs kept Seattle out of the playoffs in 1995.

The Seahawks fell to 7–9 in 1996 as Mirer was sidelined with an injury. Despite yet another disappointing finish, new team owner Paul Allen believed that his team could turn things around, and he began spending money in the off-season to make that happen. In 1997, Allen signed several key free agents, including Pro-Bowl linebacker Chad Brown and veteran quarterback Warren Moon.

Moon, who was known for his on-field intelligence and picture-perfect spirals, joined Seattle at 40 years of age. He had begun his illustrious career in the late 1970s with the

Halfback Ricky Watters ran with great intensity (pages 26-27).

Warren Moon passed for 25 touchdowns during the season.

Canadian Football League before spending 10 productive seasons with the Houston Oilers. In 1994, he joined the Minnesota Vikings and threw for more than 4,000 yards in each of his first two seasons there, earning trips to his seventh and eighth consecutive Pro Bowls.

By the end of the 1997 season, Moon had set Seattle franchise records for completions (313) and passing yards (3,678). He also became the oldest player to rush for a touchdown, to pass for 400 yards in a game, and to complete five touchdown passes in a single game.

"The most surprising thing about him is that he's still got a lot of zip on the throw," Raiders cornerback Albert Lewis said. "Once you can get past the mental limitation about his age, you'll see he hasn't lost a whole lot."

Despite Moon's heroics, the Seahawks barely reached .500, going 8–8 only by winning four games in dramatic come-from-behind fashion. Still, there were some bright spots. New addition Chad Brown led the Seahawks' defense in tackles, while speedy receiver Joey Galloway finished the season with 1,049 receiving yards and 12 touchdowns.

In 1998, Allen continued adding impact players to Seattle's roster. The most notable of those was Ricky Watters, a fiery running back formerly with Philadelphia, who ran for 1,049 yards and nine touchdowns in his first season in Seattle. "When I looked into signing Ricky, I saw that every time he played, he went 100 miles an hour," Coach Erickson said.

Despite Watters's hard running and another fine season by Galloway, the Seattle offense sputtered in 1998. Moon cracked a rib five games into the season and struggled to regain his 1997 form. After a 3–0 start, Seattle ended at 8–8.

Seattle fans and management knew that it was time to move in a new direction. 1998 had marked the 10th straight season in which Seattle missed the playoffs, and owner Paul Allen made his most aggressive move yet to change the tide of the Seahawks' fortunes. Coach Erickson was fired, and former Packers coach Mike Holmgren was brought in as Seattle's new head man.

1 9 9 9

Quarterback Jon Kitna threw for 3,346 yards to lead the Seahawks.

Holmgren had been the most sought-after coach in the NFL after dramatically reviving Green Bay's fortunes. Like the Seahawks, the Packers had gone through a nine-year playoff drought before Holmgren came in and guided them to the playoffs in only two seasons. Under his confident direction, the Packers drove all the way to a Super Bowl victory in 1996.

Allen, who was hoping for similar results in Seattle, gave Holmgren total control. As both the head coach and general manager, Holmgren would make decisions regarding drafts, trades, and player signings. "I come from the school where the personnel people and coaches work together," Holmgren said. "Everyone will be on the same page pointing at the same goal. It won't be your player . . . or my player. It will be *our* player from the Seattle Seahawks."

Holmgren dove into his new position by signing free-agent receiver Sean Dawkins. The Seahawks also made a change at quarterback, releasing Warren Moon and promoting Jon Kitna to the starting role. Defensively, Holmgren relied on Pro-Bowlers Chad Brown, Shawn Springs, and Michael Sinclair to help break Seattle's playoff jinx in 1999.

Massive defensive lineman Cortez Kennedy.

Shawn Springs provided great downfield coverage.   31

Receiver Derrick Mayes built on an impressive Seahawks career that began in 1999.

The jinx was broken, but not easily. Even though star receiver Joey Galloway sat out the first half of the season in a contract dispute, Seattle went 8–2 under Kitna. Watters helped out by rushing for 1,000 yards for the fifth straight season. In the final six games of the season, though, Seattle's offense went into a tailspin, scoring only two touchdowns. Still, a 9–7 record was good enough to win the AFC Western Division title and secure the team's first playoff berth in 11 seasons.

The Seahawks' long-awaited playoff run was short-lived. They fell to Miami, 20–17, as Kitna was battered relentlessly by Dolphins defenders. "We had difficulties running the football, and we had difficulties with our pass protection," lamented Holmgren. "We just couldn't get anything going."

With Coach Holmgren at the helm, the Seahawks' rollercoaster ride seems to be heading upward once again. The addition of speedy University of Alabama running back Shaun Alexander should continue to boost Seattle's rise. After finally breaking into the playoff picture in 1999, it may only be a matter of time before the Seahawks add a shiny Super Bowl trophy to the beauty of the Emerald City.